INDEX

Hezbollah in Syria

The involvement of Hezbollah in the Syrian civil war has become one of the most well-known basic facts about the conflict. The group's intervention inside Syria first gained widespread public attention in the battle for Qusayr in Homs province—bordering Lebanon—in late May 2013, clearly playing a leading role ahead of the regular Syrian armed forces.

The most notable subsequent campaigns for Hezbollah in Syria have included clearing out rebel strongholds in rural Damascus province, such as Nabk and Yabroud, fighting in East Ghouta areas like al-Mliha, clearing out the rebels from Homs city, and the long-standing attempt by the Assad regime to encircle Aleppo city and destroy rebel forces by siege.

The Hezbollah fighters are engaging in an obligatory defensive jihad, above all for the Sayyida Zaynab shrine in Damascus, and they are fighting "takfiri" forces—that is, Sunni extremists who denounce as disbelievers/apostates others who profess to be Muslim, particularly those of non-Sunni sects like the Shi'a. These forces are also portrayed as a threat to Lebanon itself, not wholly without justification, considering that in Sunni jihadi discourse Lebanon is regarded as a part of al-Sham (greater Syria) and the same battlefield as the Syrian jihad. Indeed, some Lebanese Sunni jihadists have taken the opportunity to expand into Syria, which could allow them to grow in strength and conduct more sophisticated operations inside Lebanon in the future.

Beyond the direct role of supplying fighters to participate in combat operations, Hezbollah has also had an important part in establishing and coordinating the wider Shi'i jihad in Syria, which has now expanded its recruitment pool to include a contingent of Pakistani Shi'a fighters known as Liwa Zaynibiyoun. Hezbollah's role as coordinator and advisor in the wider jihad fits in with its status as the chief proxy of Iran in the region, necessitating the preservation of the Assad regime to keep together the core of the Iranian-led "resistance" bloc.

Any notions of demoralization and doubts within Hezbollah about the validity of the war effort are quite mistaken for the time being. This is so despite the regime's recent losses in Idlib province to the rebels and in eastern Homs province to IS—which have seen the regime lose control of its entire eastern border with Iraq, the historic city of Palmyra that has played a notable role in the attempt by some pro-regime factions to stress distinct Syrian identity, and vital oil and gas reserves that have allowed the regime to distribute cheap fuel and electricity in areas under its control. These losses have brought to light some unease on the regime side regarding the viability of a long war to reunite the country under its rule, as well as concerns about overreliance on foreign forces.

For Hezbollah, the perspective is quite different. First, and perhaps most broadly, in having intervened and helped the regime secure several vital areas in western Syria, the tables have been turned. No longer is the Syrian regime a regional power projecting its influence into Lebanon through support for "resistance" factions, but instead Hezbollah is projecting its influence onto the territories of a Syrian regime unable to support itself without foreign aid and manpower.

Other perceived benefits for Hezbollah include the potential to open up a new front against Israel in the Golan area in keeping with the group's projection of itself as a "resistance" force. In turn, Israel has recognized the threat through airstrikes targeting Hezbollah in Syria—the most-well known incident taking out Imad Mughniyah's son Jihad in Quneitra in January 2015.

Further, as an adherent of Iran's revolutionary ideology of absolute wilayat al-faqih ("guardianship of the jurist," devised by Ayatollah Khomeini), Hezbollah is devoted to spreading these ideals among the Shi'a worldwide. One of the ways to accomplish this goal is to portray itself and Iran as the leaders and protectors of the Shi'a in the region. Though Shi'i clerical views on fighting in Syria have by no means been monolithic (with lack of support from both Ayatollah Sistani and Muqtada al-Sadr), notions of shrine defense have an undeniable popular appeal; and with the rise of IS in both Syria and Iraq with its genocidal views towards the Shi'a, the idea that—like it or not—Shi'a must seek the help of Iran and aligned forces to combat the existential threat has gained increasing currency.

In a similar vein, on the home front in Lebanon, Hizballah has the ability to feed a narrative to minority populations in particular that only it can protect them from the threats over the border. Christians above all have been a key target of this Hezbollah outreach, and emphasis on solidarity with Christians in Syria and Lebanon has been a strong theme of its discourse. The result is a degree of success in the appeal of the Hezbollah-affiliated Saraya al-Muqawama

("Resistance Brigades") in Christian localities such as Ras Baalbek along the border with Syria. Lacking competition from its March 14 rivals to offer military protection to these communities, Hezbollah finds many residents of these areas willing to turn to it for support, whatever the suspicions regarding Hezbollah's relationship with the Syrian regime, the nature of its intervention in Syria, and past bitter memories of the Lebanese civil war.

In short, from Hezbollah's standpoint of extending its influence at home and abroad, the intervention in the Syrian civil war should be seen as more of a net benefit, in spite of the casualties the group has sustained in the fighting. There is no sign of internal fragmentation here comparable to the growing (though by no means yet fatal) hints of trouble within the Assad regime's constituencies regarding the war as the defensive lines increasingly retreat from peripheries to consolidate the rump state. To consider the issue of Hezbollah casualties in greater depth and its impact, it is necessary to examine the culture of "martyrdom" surrounding the fallen Hezbollah fighters, both in the online realm and on the ground in Lebanon.

The total number of Hezbollah "martyrs" killed in Syria remains a controversial issue. Numbers could be inflated or minimized for a variety of reasons. For example, critics of Hezbollah within Lebanon may overstate the number of fighters killed to make out that Syria is proving to be Hezbollah's "Vietnam"–a lengthy campaign with numerous casualties but ultimately no strategic gains. In this case, estimates for slain Hizballah fighters are regularly given as at least 1,000. Conversely, Hezbollah members and pro-Hezbollah sources may understate the number of casualties, aware of some of the sensitivities regarding numbers of dead. Sources on both sides may overstate the number of Hezbollah fighters in Syria too, exaggerating for their own polemical reasons the role of Hezbollah in the war–the pro-Hezbollah side to portray the group as the vital salvation for Syria in the face of the deemed takfiri threat, the anti-Hezbollah side to lambast what is seen as the disproportionate attention given to Sunni foreign fighters.

The axis of resistance is an Iran-led alliance of state and non-state actors in the Middle East that seeks to confront Western interests in the region, namely those of the United States and Israel. Historically, this alliance has included the Assad regime in Syria and Lebanese Hezbollah. In recent years, Iran has also cultivated Iraqi Shi'a militants as the newest members of this alliance. Aside from shared regional objectives, another pillar of the axis is shared support. Iran provides extensive material, financial, training, and logistical assistance to its regional partners. For example, Iran has supplied Hezbollah with as much as $200 million each year.

After Hezbollah's 2006 war with Israel, Iran and Syria rearmed Hezbollah with vastly expanded and more sophisticated weaponry. Much of this support has passed through Syria, making it the primary hub in Iran's power projection in the Levant. The war in Syria presents a significant, even existential, threat to this strategic alliance by endangering one of its primary members and the chief conduit for Iranian support to Hezbollah. At the same time, Iran cannot afford to lose its most important foothold in the Levant, and Hezbollah cannot risk losing its access to critical Iranian and Syrian support. Maintaining the axis of resistance is also a matter of great ideological importance for Iran and its commitment to exporting its Islamic revolutionary principles. For all of these reasons, Iran will go to great lengths to preserve its foothold in Syria.

The Assad regime has relied heavily on its allies, Iran and Hezbollah, for support. Hezbollah has augmented Iran's considerable investment in Syria by providing capabilities that its partners lack. Hezbollah trainers and advisers are well suited to assist pro-regime forces because they speak Arabic (unlike their Iranian counterparts) and have combat experience fighting Israel in southern Lebanon. The Syrian army consists mainly of heavy, mechanized units, which have had difficulty operating in urban environments against lightly armed guerilla forces.

Hezbollah fighters, therefore, offer capabilities that complement the Assad regime, including light infantry, reconnaissance, and snipers. Since 2006, Hezbollah fighters have trained in Lebanon and Iran in tactics of both offensive and defensive urban warfare. Hezbollah can also provide additional training and combat manpower at a time when pro-regime forces are stretched from years of fighting.

Hezbollah chief Hassan Nasrallah called Syria the "backbone" of the resistance in his May 2013 speech, in which he openly acknowledged Hezbollah's involvement in Syria on behalf of the Assad regime.

The Assad regime has played a vital role in the transfer of weapons, equipment, and money from Iran to Hezbollah in Lebanon. The Iranian regime has flown large numbers of weapons to Damascus, including thousands of rockets as well as accurate and long-range surface-to-surface missiles. Iran has used civilian aircraft and Turkish airspace for these flights, although the air routes have shifted to Iraq on account of more stringent Turkish controls and Iraq's own challenges in policing its airspace.

Syria's importance to Hezbollah is not limited to its role as a conduit for financial and material support. The Assad regime has provided safe haven for Hezbollah training camps and weapons storage. Some of these training camps in Syria are located near suspected chemical weapons depots, a development that has worried U.S. officials.

Hezbollah's Strategy in Syria

Hezbollah has become more deeply involved in Syria as the conflict has protracted, given these mutual interests. Hezbollah's support for Assad seeks to achieve three broad objectives. First, Hezbollah seeks to preserve the Axis of resistance by shoring up the military capabilities of the Assad regime. It is doing this through the provision of training and assistance, and more recently through direct combat involvement.

Second, Hezbollah also seeks to retain access to Iranian and Syrian material support by securing the lines of communication that run from Damascus to Lebanon from any rebel interference. This has brought it in conflict with rebel groups. For example, the major campaign in al-Qusayr, was an effort to cut off rebel supply lines that both threatened Lebanese Shi'a communities in Syria and endangered to Hezbollah's own lines of communication in the Bekaa valley of Lebanon.

Third, the group also seeks to prevent the emergence of Sunni-dominated regime in Syria should Assad fall. Many Shi'a Lebanese are concerned about the rise of "takfiri" groups (a term indicating extreme Sunni organizations) within Syria and the potential for spillover into Lebanon. This has incentivized Hezbollah to fight these groups in Syria to prevent them from strengthening and expanding into Lebanon. As the conflict has taken a more sectarian turn, Hezbollah has also portrayed itself as the defender of the Shi'a in Syria. It has positioned its forces in defense of important Shi'a religious sites, most notably the Sayyida Zeinab shrine in Damascus. Hezbollah has also sought to protect Lebanese Shi'a living in Syria, particularly those along the border with Lebanon.

Hezbollah sided with the Assad regime within weeks of the first protests in Syria, Hassan Nasrallah publicly declared his organization's backing of Assad in May 2013, even before the uprising turned violent. Hezbollah rhetorical support for Syrian regime has remained constant throughout the conflict; however, the group's involvement on the ground has evolved as the fighting has protracted.

Hezbollah's activities in Syria in the early years of the conflict were limited in size and scope primarily to advisory and support roles. This was likely a result of the organization's reluctance to get drawn into the fighting in Syria for fear of its consequences for detrimental effects that such involvement might have for Lebanon's stability and for Hezbollah's standing. Moreover, the uprising had not yet metastasized to the scale and scope it has now reached at the beginning

The nature of Hezbollah's activities has obscured information on the group's early involvement in Syria. Accusations of Hezbollah's activities in Syria on behalf of the regime surfaced in the fall of 2011. For example, in September 2011, Lebanese media reported that several Hezbollah fighters were killed in Syria, where they were assisting the Assad regime's crackdown on protesters.

One Syrian government defector accused the regime of using Hezbollah snipers against demonstrators, and claimed that fighters from the Lebanese militant group were fighting alongside Assad's forces in Zabadani. Other reports claimed that scores of Hezbollah fighters were killed in clashes with Free Syrian Army fighters in Homs and Damascus in late 2011.

It is difficult to verify the validity of these claims. Many of these stories appear in anti-regime media outlets or are based on single-source reporting from opposition sources. Still, rumors of Hezbollah's involvement did elicit a response from Hassan Nasrallah, who called it "absolutely untrue" that Hezbollah had sent fighters to Syria.

More credible evidence of Hezbollah's role in Syria came to light in the second half of 2012. U.S officials publicly acknowledged Hezbollah's involvement in the Syrian conflict in August 2012. According to a U.S. treasury designation, Hezbollah has since early 2011 "directly trained Syrian government personnel inside Syria and has facilitated the training of Syrian forces by Iran's Islamic Revolutionary Guard Corps - Qods Force (IRGC-QF). Hezbollah also has played a substantial role in efforts to expel Syrian opposition forces from areas within Syria."

This official designation lent credence to other reports that members of Hezbollah's Unit 910, an elite commando force that conducts clandestine activities outside of Lebanon, had assisted the Syrian military in and around Homs during the summer of 2012.

Burials of Hezbollah fighters killed in Syria also bolstered U.S. and opposition claims of the Lebanese militant group's growing role in the uprising. In the summer of 2012, Hezbollah's fighters killed in Syria were quietly buried in Lebanon. These burials occurred often with few formalities, as Hezbollah officials remained unwilling to publicly acknowledge their involvement in Syria. The public funeral of a senior Hezbollah commander, Ali Hussein Nassif, in the Bekaa valley in early October was a departure from previous burials because it drew large crowds, including high-ranking Hezbollah officials.

Hezbollah claimed that Nassif was killed doing his "jihadist duties," a phrase used to obscure the location and activities of Hezbollah martyrs. Lebanese officials, however, acknowledged that Nassif's body had been transferred from Syria, where he was killed in late September.

According to reports by Free Syrian Army fighters and anti-regime activists, Nassif was killed south of al-Qusayr when an improvised explosive device (ieD) targeted his convoy. It is unclear what Nassif was doing in Syria, but the reported location of his death was an area where opposition members accused Hezbollah of operating alongside Syrian forces in an effort to clear rebel pockets.

The public funerals of Hezbollah members put the organization in a difficult position. Facing growing scrutiny over the group's role in Syria, Nasrallah denied that his organization was fighting alongside the Assad regime in a speech in mid-October 2012. Yet, he did acknowledge indirectly that Hezbollah members were fighting in Syria, but that they were there of their own accord to defend Lebanese Shi'a living in villages near the border.

Escalating role in 2013 Hezbollah's role in Syria shifted dramatically in early 2013 from what was primarily an advisory mission to one in which Hezbollah forces assumed a direct combat role, operating in larger numbers alongside Syrian military and paramilitary forces. They also expanded their efforts to train a reorganized pro-Assad paramilitary force. The extent of Hezbollah's contributions remains murky, but their impact on the battlefield in 2013 is without question. Late 2012 and early 2013 was low point for the Assad regime and its Iranian backers.

The pace of fighting had strained the Assad regime's military capabilities and there was increasing pessimism about the survivability of the Assad regime. Rebel forces were gaining ground in Aleppo and the north. The conflict was becoming increasingly sectarian, and al-Qaeda aligned groups like Jabhat al-nusra were assuming a more prominent role in Syria. Iran had also suffered important losses in Syria. In August 2012, Syrian rebels captured forty-eight members of Iran's Islamic Revolutionary Guards Corps-Qods Force (IRGC-QF), who were released a month later in exchange for two thousand prisoners held by the Assad regime.

The February 2013 assassination of senior Qods Force General Hassan Shateri in Syria was another critical blow. Iran increased its commitment to the Assad regime during this time, stepping up its efforts to reverse the situation in Syria.

IRGC-QF commander Qassem Soleimani made regular visits to Damascus to personally oversee the operations. Also present at Soleimani's headquarters in Damascus were the top commanders of Syria's military, a Hezbollah commander, and a coordinator for Iraq's Shi'a militants. Iran also increased the pace of its supply flights and ramped up its presence of IRGC-QF advisers across the country.

The Assad regime, at the urging of Iran, adjusted its strategy for the coming year and sought to focus on several key areas rather than trying to flight conduct operations against multiple fronts simultaneously. The regime intended to concentrate first on Damascus and the areas that link the capital to Homs and the coast in order to consolidate control over these areas before pushing further north and east. The regime's focus also included securing the areas along the Lebanon-Syria border.

Hezbollah also shared this goal, as rebel gains threatened its own strongholds in the Bekaa valley. The Syrian regime also embarked on a reorganization of its paramilitary forces in late 2012. A number of pro-Assad militias operated in Syria, namely the Jaysh al-shaabi (Popular army) and the Shabiha. These groups were primarily alawite, drawn from local communities as a neighborhood-watch force. Many of these groups were folded into a newly created National Defense Force (NDF), a national paramilitary force intended to resemble Iran's basij force. Indeed, brigadier General Hossein Hamedani, the former Basij deputy commander, was involved in the efforts to stand up the paramilitary force. Other sources say Hamedani also directs operations in Syria and oversees Iranian arms shipments to Hezbollah.

The NDF is comprised mostly of Alawites and regime loyalists, like the Jaysh al-Shaabi or shabiha. Yet, the NDF has a more formalized and functional structure and its members are licensed, trained, equipped, and paid by the regime.The NDF numbered around 50,000-60,000 by mid-2013, and was set to grow to 100,000.

As Iran's increased commitment to Assad's survival, Hezbollah also stepped up its activities in Syria on behalf of the Assad regime. This was likely the result of Iranian encouragement as well as mutual interests. One avenue for Hezbollah's deepened involvement was its role in the creation and expansion of the NDF.

Hezbollah operatives have trained NDF members throughout Syria, including in Latakia, Homs, Damascus, and Aleppo. As previously mentioned, Hezbollah's combat experience in unconventional and urban warfare, light Infantry capability, and common language make it an ideal training force for Syrian paramilitaries.

Hezbollah's Known Activities in Syria

Hezbollah has made a significant commitment of forces to Syria, out determining the actual number of personnel involved is difficult. The high reported number of Hezbollah forces estimated to have been committed to Syria is about 10,000, but this likely reflects the total rotated through Syria, not the number present at any one time. The French foreign minister provided a more reasonable estimate of 3,000-4,000 in May 2013 during the height of the battle in Qusayr.

In September 2013, Reuters cited "regional security officials" as providing an estimate of 2,000-4,000. Types of units and troops sent to Syria include "elite and special forces," and "reservists." Given the scope of reported Hizbollah activity in Syria, including types of missions and areas of operation, up to 4,000 fighters seems a reasonable estimate.

Based on videos of purported Hezbollah combatants in Syria, they resemble regular soldiers. They are uniformed, have load bearing equipment, and in some cases wear protective vests. Weapons and equipment also seen with purported Hizb Allah forces in Syria include standard light infantry weapons (assault rifles, general purpose machine guns), anti-tank guided missiles (ATGM) and rocket-propelled grenades (RPG), truck-mounted heavy machine guns ("Dushkas"), light mortars, and recoilless rifles. Hizb Allah reportedly operated regime armored vehicles in the fighting in Qusayr, but this was likely a situation in which Hizb Allah forces were operating with regime regular armored units.

The organization of Hezbollah forces in Syria is unclear. One report, citing a "regional security source," indicated that Hezbollah functions with a command structure including Islamic Revolutionary Guard Corps (IRGC) and Syrian Army personnel and has been given specific geographic areas of responsibility. Based on the different geographic fronts where they are fighting, Hizb Allah forces are probably organized on a territorial basis with separate commands for forces in Damascus and its suburbs, Aleppo city and Aleppo Province, and Homs Province.

Hezbollah is one component of the diverse forces mobilized by the regime. These forces include: regime regulars from the army, air force, air defense force, and navy; irregular forces of the National Defense Force (NDF); allied forces from Iraq; and possibly some Iranian combat forces in small numbers.

Hezbollah has brought important capabilities to the war on the regime's side. Its forces in Syria are essentially light infantry that can be depended on to execute both offensive and defensive missions in areas important to the regime. They have learned to cooperate with regime heavy forces including armor, artillery, and air units, and to work effectively with regime irregulars and allies.

Hezbollah has conducted four types of military missions in Syria:
– A training mission for regime regular and irregular forces in urban and counterinsurgency operations;
– A combat advisory role with regime regulars and irregulars;
– "Corseting" operations, providing a key reinforcing component of allied Iraqi/Shi`a forces, such as in the Damascus suburbs;
– Direct combat operations on key battlefields, as seen in Qusayr.

All of these roles have been important to regime successes since at least June 2013. Hezbollah has been involved in both joint and combined offensive and defensive operations. It participates in joint operations with regime heavy forces (armor and artillery), air force units, and surface-to-surface missile units. Joint and combined operations are a standard approach; in combat operations, Hezbollah forces are frequently seen and reported working with regime and allied forces.

Based largely on opposition reporting, Hezbollah has been involved in direct combat and corseting operations in eight areas within Syria, and in corseting and advisory operations in three more. Reports posted by Syrian opposition elements reveal more than 80 specific locations where Hezbollah is said to have been involved in military actions.

Hezbollah's combat performance in Syria has been at least fair. Its forces have the training and experience to conduct attacks and defensive actions with skill, and they have demonstrated a willingness to accept the casualties necessary to achieve their objectives. Nevertheless, Hezbollah's forces have not always proved successful in offensive actions, suffering some tactical setbacks in the fighting for Qusayr, and may have failed in some defensive actions in the eastern Damascus suburbs during heavy fighting there in late November 2013.

The 2013 Qusayr campaign is a case in point. The Syrian regime's and Hezbollah's operation to retake control of Qusayr began in April 2013, and the assault on the city, which began on May 19, lasted 17 days, even with regime and Hezbollah forces having the advantage of firepower and the ability to isolate the city. Hezbollah was apparently surprised by the level of resistance offered by the rebels, the rebels' extensive use of mines and improvised explosive devices (IEDs), and was unfamiliar with the area of operations.

Hezbollah is making a difference in Syria, but not everywhere and not yet decisively. Its forces have become the regime's "fire brigade," employed in critical areas and actions. It has helped to keep the regime in the war, and arguably it has helped reverse the course of the conflict. It has restored the regime's ability to conduct significant offensive operations, and has been instrumental to regime successes in Homs Province, Aleppo Province and Damascus and its suburbs.

The military environment in Syria presents serious challenges to Hezbollah. One of the group's strengths in southern Lebanon has always been its intimate understanding of the terrain. Hezbollah personnel may have had some familiarity with the terrain on the Syrian side of the border, but beyond a few miles they would have had little knowledge, and in the depth of Syria, where they now find themselves operating, they have effectively no knowledge. Although they are now gaining familiarity in the areas in which they are deployed, this process takes time, and each movement into a new area requires learning. The terrain in Syria is also militarily undeveloped, unlike southern Lebanon where Hezbollah has created an elaborate military infrastructure of fortifications, obstacles, demolitions, command facilities, observation posts, storage facilities, and barracks, comprising hundreds of positions.

Hezbollah personnel are involved in both urban and rural fighting over long distances and on multiple fronts. The distances involved and the size and complexity of the urban environments in Syria are unprecedented for the organization. Hezbollah's previous major ground combat experience was limited mostly to a relatively small area of southern Lebanon adjacent to the Israeli border. It is now fighting on three or four different fronts separated by tens, and, in the case of the Aleppo front, hundreds of miles. Its urban combat experience was largely limited to the towns and villages of southern Lebanon, while in Syria it is involved in close combat in the sprawling neighborhoods of major cities such as Damascus, Homs and Aleppo.

The human terrain, or the sectarian map, of the Syrian theater is more complex than Hezbollah faces in southern Lebanon, the latter of which has a strong Shi`a majority. Unlike in its previous conflicts with Israel, Hezbollah is operating in some areas that have a hostile Sunni population that supports its opponents. In these areas, Hezbollah is the "occupier" and faces armed "resistance."

Moreover, the Sunni rebels in Syria are not the enemy who Hezbollah planned to fight. Hezbollah's careful study of the Israel Defense Forces (IDF) and meticulous preparation for fighting it avail Hezbollah little against the rebels in Syria. These opponents are diverse irregulars with little in the way of formal organization, heavy forces, and established doctrine. In some ways, they are like Hezbollah itself, with a strong ideological foundation and a deep commitment to their mission.

Additionally, unlike Lebanon, Hezbollah in Syria is involved in complex coalition warfare including joint and combined operations. The nature of the war being fought by the regime demands that Hezbollah work with forces as different as those of the regime's air force and the irregular Iraqi volunteers such as the Abu Fadl al-Abbas Brigade.

In terms of challenges in Syria, Hezbollah is conducting operations (including offensive ones), and not just fighting tactical battles. This is warfare of a different kind than it has waged against the IDF, involving larger formations, longer periods of time, in more complex maneuvers, and placing more demands—in terms of planning and command and control—on the combat forces and on supporting elements (especially intelligence and logistics). All of this is certainly a challenge to Hezbollah's command and control capabilities, which were built for an almost "set-piece" battle with the well-understood IDF.

Hezbollah is a learning organization. It studies its opponents and draws conclusions from its combat operations. Lessons it may have learned, re-learned, or had emphasized in the Syrian conflict likely involve:

— The role of firepower in offensive and defensive operations, including its application, coordination, and effects;
— The requirements of conducting sustained combat operations over a broad area in terms of planning, command and control, logistics, rotation of forces and personnel;

– The complexities and challenges of working with allied regular and irregular forces;
– The high cost of offensive operations in manpower and resources;
– The conduct of company/battalion size offensive operations;
– The planning and conduct of complex operations.

Hezbollah is gaining command and control experience at the operational and tactical levels. It is raising a new crop of fighters and leaders with combat experience. It is hardening its personnel and units for the rigors of combat, likely increasing their cohesion and resilience. It is improving individual and small unit weapons and tactical skills. It is gaining experience in the collection and use of tactical and operational intelligence. As a result of its involvement in Syria, Hezbollah will be better prepared to fight in Lebanon. With an improved understanding of the strengths and weaknesses of Sunni irregular forces and increased experience in combat, its superiority over potential opponents in Lebanon, including the Lebanese Armed Forces, will be enhanced.

Nevertheless, Hezbollah is also incurring costs from its Syria intervention. In addition to casualties, it has become the target of Sunni elements operating in Lebanon, which have penetrated to the very heart of the organization in southern Beirut. Its participation in the conflict has contributed to rising Sunni-Shi`a tensions in Lebanon. Once the darling of the Arab world, Hezbollah is now seen, in at least some quarters, as an enemy of Sunnis.

The fighting in Syria should improve Hezbollah's ability to fight the IDF, but the improvement will be limited, and some of what Hezbollah learns in Syria will be irrelevant to fighting the IDF. In the fighting in Syria, Hezbollah enjoys significant advantages over the rebels, including: regime firepower, a secure base area, extensive logistics, robust command and control, and the opportunity for operational maneuver. In a war with Israel, these advantages would be with the IDF. Nevertheless, some improvement in combat performance and coordination of forces should be expected, including a capability for offensive actions at the company level.

Yet, it is in Syria where Hezbollah's role has the greatest military and political implications. Hezbollah's intervention has been instrumental in preserving the regime. It is probably the best force on the battlefield at this stage of the Syrian war. It has proven itself a reliable and effective ally. It is willing to accept the political risks and the casualties of a prolonged and essentially open ended intervention.

Hezbollah's Russian Military Education

For the first time in its history, Hezbollah is conducting offensive maneuver warfare as part of its operations in Syria. The Russian intervention is only enhancing that experience, likely giving the group important lessons for future conflicts.

Thus far, Hezbollah has long followed a strategy of defense and attrition in hostilities against its main enemy, Israel -- an approach that many high-ranking officers in the Israel Defense Forces (IDF) liked to call "not losing." Taking into account Israel's manpower and technological advantages, this strategy focused on prolonging the fighting as much as possible, maintaining home-front attrition by firing rockets on Israeli population centers, and increasing the costs of IDF ground maneuvers in southern Lebanon. Hezbollah displayed this defensive mindset during the 2006 war when it hid rockets and fighters in elaborate networks of underground fortifications and areas of dense vegetation that Israeli officers dubbed "nature reserves." The group believed that as long as it did not crumble, it could claim that it survived a war with the mighty IDF, which according to its narrative was actually a win. The Syria war has changed this defensive paradigm, however.

In Syria, Hezbollah has had to shift its main objectives to taking over territory and maintaining control over it, all while fighting quasi-conventional forces that use guerrilla tactics. Against the IDF, the group was accustomed to fighting in small units on familiar terrain, but now it is deploying hundreds of fighters in complex offensive operations on unfamiliar territory. For Hezbollah's commanders and fighters, such experience can change their views on the most effective way to win a battle, and Russia's involvement means that they are learning such lessons from one of the best militaries in the world.

From the start, Russia has depended on Syrian, Iranian, Hezbollah, and other Shiite forces to get the job done on the ground. Given the complexity of the campaign and Moscow's desire to avoid perceptions of failure, Russian forces are probably maintaining very close cooperation with their partners to make sure they are executing their missions. Reports indicate that joint Hezbollah-Russian operations rooms have been established in Latakia and Damascus, while Hezbollah and Iranian personnel apparently helped recover a downed Russian pilot in November. Moscow still seems reluctant to add significant ground forces to the fight, so it will need to strengthen such coordination even further.

On the macro level, Hezbollah will be exposed to Russian military thought, which entails sophisticated operational concepts and advanced military planning skills. The Russian military has ample experience in conducting different types of operations, including counterinsurgency and conventional campaigns. Consider this scenario: a Russian commander sits with Hezbollah, Iranian, and Syrian commanders and lays out the military strategy for the Syria campaign. He talks about the objectives, the timeframe to achieve these objectives, and the priorities in the fight. He then emphasizes which assets can be instrumental in battle, and perhaps offers important lessons from past operations such as the counterinsurgency campaign in Chechnya. For Hezbollah, this will be the first time it will be able to watch how a first-tier military plans a fighting campaign.

Learning processes such as these happen all the time. For example, Syria's experience as part of the American coalition during Operation Desert Storm in 1991 transformed its war strategy altogether. After witnessing firsthand the effects of a U.S. Air Land battle and the efficiency of precision-guided munitions, the Syrian military correctly inferred that Israel could employ some of the same munitions and tactics. Accordingly, the regime shifted its focus from thinking about how to conquer the Golan Heights to a more defensive strategy that entailed restructuring certain units and procuring/developing multiple antitank, fire, and improvised explosive device capabilities.

In addition, when actors are planning a joint military campaign involving simultaneous air and ground offensives, they usually share intelligence with each other, and the current war is no exception -- the Russians have probably shared battlefield intelligence with Hezbollah in Syria and exposed the group to its intelligence assets. This would not be the first time they have done so. During the 2006 Lebanon war, a joint Syrian-Russian intelligence post located in Syrian territory passed intelligence reports to Hezbollah.

More generally, the group may be getting a good look at how Russian analysts combine signal, visual, and open-source intelligence to present a better picture of the enemy and the battlefield. This likely includes the use of satellite imagery, aerial footage from Orlan-10 drones, advanced signals intelligence capabilities, and electronic warfare elements. Such observations would be particularly valuable because Hezbollah has not had much experience in maximizing visual intelligence from drones and incorporating it with other intelligence.

Working with the Russians will also help the group learn how to execute complex offensive operations in urban environments. In previous conflicts, Hezbollah tactics focused on guerrilla warfare, with small units responsible for defending their villages or blocking IDF movements. This approach does not apply to many battles in Syria, where Hezbollah has often had to deploy much larger units in offensive operations in tandem with artillery and aerial assets. Russian forces have extensive urban warfare experience, so they likely have many pointers for the group, including how to organize an effective command-and-control structure, how to choose different weapons for different scenarios, how to create additional targets after entering a battlefield, and how to maintain logistical routes.

In Chechnya, for example, the Russians formed "Storm" detachments composed of snipers, soldiers with automatic weapons, forward observers, and reconnaissance personnel -- an approach meant to maximize mobility and flexibility. They also used numerous rocket launchers (e.g., the TOS-1 mobile thermobaric multiple rocket launcher and the man-portable RPO-A Shmel) while maneuvering inside the Chechen capital of Grozny, indicating good coordination between different elements. Discussing these tactics with experienced Russian commanders could give Hezbollah deep insight into properly task-organizing its forces, effectively coordinating disparate elements on the battlefield, and other matters -- an invaluable benefit despite the group's lesser training and equipment compared to Russian troops.

When military commanders experience a long, difficult campaign, their thoughts inevitably stray to potential future conflicts. This often means translating the lessons they have learned into new strategies and new tactics -- and new approaches to military procurement and training. Hezbollah commanders in Syria are no doubt already thinking about such issues, and fighting alongside the Russians could greatly affect their conclusions.

On the strategic level, the group no longer seems married to its "not losing" mindset, instead focusing on ways to achieve perceived victories early in a given conflict. In 2011, for example, Hezbollah leader Hassan Nasrallah mentioned that his forces plan to infiltrate Israel's northern border during the next war in order to conquer settlements in the Galilee, and he has repeated this sentiment since then. This is a major departure from the group's traditional defensive paradigm, and conversations with Russian commanders could cement that shift and help the group further develop its offensive strategies.

On the tactical level, Hezbollah now has a front-row seat to watch the variety of weapons systems and equipment the Russians are bringing to bear in Syria, some of which it has never seen before. Thus, the group can learn how to use its existing weapons (some of which are Russian made) more effectively and examine systems it might want to procure in the future. Recently, for example, reports indicated that Hezbollah has acquired SA-22 surface-to-air missiles. Russia has brought the same system into Syria -- if these weapons are put into use under the supervision of joint operations rooms, Hezbollah personnel could get a better sense of how to operate the system's radar and deal with multiple targets at the same time. Similarly, they will witness how Russian ground forces use rocket systems such as the TOS-1 and RPO-A Shmel, which have already been spotted in Syria and might seem useful to the group in a future war with Israel. Even experience with superior Russian versions of basic equipment could prove crucial, including night-vision goggles, tactical vests, and medical supplies.

Almost three months have passed since Moscow began its campaign in Syria, signaling its strong commitment to preserving the Assad regime. Given that Russia and Hezbollah are not retreating anytime soon, the group's learning process will continue. Furthermore, Russia is reportedly in the process of increasing its military so Hezbollah may get the chance to learn additional lessons.

Recent history has also shown that whatever Hezbollah learns, its partners in crime will soon follow suit. Numerous terrorist organizations have studied and implemented the group's military tactics -- in some cases, Hezbollah even sent trainers to help certain proxies upgrade their capabilities. For example, Hezbollah-trained Shiite militias demonstrated such tactics against American soldiers in Iraq prior to the U.S. withdrawal. High-ranking Hezbollah veterans also reportedly trained Houthi forces in Yemen, who are now showing significant capabilities in their fight against the Arab coalition. And in Gaza, terrorist organizations such as Hamas and Palestinian Islamic Jihad have long implemented Hezbollah strategies in the political and the military realms.

Moreover, as Hezbollah learns from the Russians, it will become even more capable relative to the Lebanese Armed Forces, which are already weaker than the group in terms of fighting experience and weapons. Tilting the balance of power further in Hezbollah's favor is a dangerous prospect given Lebanon's atmosphere of heightened instability and factional tension.

Regarding Israel, it is important to note that while Hezbollah is gaining valuable experience in Syria, the enemies they face there are far weaker than the IDF. Jabhat al-Nusra, the Islamic State, and various rebel factions all have their strengths, but they do not present the same challenges as a war against a well-trained military with a highly capable air force, navy, and army, all of whom know Hezbollah very well. The group will learn important lessons, but implementing them will be very challenging, especially when the rival is the IDF.

As Russia entered the Syrian theatre in September, Nasrallah told al-Manar Television that Moscow was "playing a positive role that will have a positive outcome, God willing." The Russian military education that Hezbollah will receive in the coming months will only reinforce the group's optimism -- and capabilities.

Hezbollah in Iraq

As Sunni militants from the Islamic State of Iraq and al-Sham (ISIS) captured Mosul and set their sights on Baghdad, Hezbollah leader Hassan Nasrallah offered to send fighters to Iraq to help turn the jihadist tide. In Syria, the Lebanese Shiite group's forces have already deployed in large numbers over the past several years and made all the difference in the Assad regime's battle for survival. In Iraq, Hezbollah would likely dispatch only small numbers of trainers and special operators. Yet given the group's past special operations and training activities in Iraq and its close ties with Iran's elite Qods Force, even a modest deployment would likely have a significant impact.

On June 17, Nasrallah pledged, "*We are ready to sacrifice martyrs in Iraq five times more than what we sacrificed in Syria in order to protect shrines,*' noting that Iraqi holy sites "*are much more important*' than Shiite shrines in Syria. To be sure, Hezbollah is heavily invested in the Syria war and will probably increase its presence there as Iraqi Shiites leave to defend their homeland from ISIS. Yet the group can make a significant contribution to the Shiite counteroffensive in Iraq without having to redirect many of its operatives or resources from Syria.

During the last Iraq war, Hezbollah effectively used a limited number of special operations personnel to train Iraqi Shiite militants and support sporadic special operations targeting coalition forces. As a 2009 Australian government report concluded, "*Hezbollah has established an insurgent capability in Iraq, engaging in assassinations, kidnappings and bombings. The Hezbollah units have been set up with the encouragement and resources of Iran's Revolutionary Guards al-Qods Brigades.*" The Qods Force will likely request a similar initiative to aid the Shiite-led government in Baghdad today, turning these capabilities against ISIS with potentially far-reaching benefits for Iraqi Shiite militias.

Beginning in 2003, Iran's Qods Force requested Hezbollah's services to help increase Tehran's influence in Iraq. To this end, Hezbollah created Unit 3800, whose sole purpose was to support Iraqi Shiite militant groups targeting multinational forces there. According to U.S. intelligence, Unit 3800 sent a small number of personnel to Iraq to train hundreds of fighters in-country, while others were brought to Lebanon for more advanced training. Hezbollah also provided funds and weapons to Iraqi militias, but its most dangerous contribution was in the realm of special operations. According to a 2010

Pentagon report, the group gave these militias *"the training, tactics and technology to conduct kidnappings [and] small unit tactical operations,"* and to *"employ sophisticated improvised explosive devices (IEDs), incorporating lessons learned from operations in Southern Lebanon."*

The most prominent example of how this training helped the militias was probably the January 20, 2007, attack on the Joint Coordination Center in Karbala, which resulted in the deaths of four American soldiers. That well-executed operation was thoroughly planned with the help of the Qods Force and Hezbollah, as determined later through the capture of one of Hezbollah's best trainers in Iraq, Ali Musa Daqduq.

Daqduq was heavily involved in training tactical units of Iraqi Shiites and even took part in some of the operations they conducted. He was also responsible for planning other operations such as the aborted kidnapping of a British soldier, and gave specific instructions to those he trained about the use of IEDs. Moreover, while operating in Iraq, he dealt directly with the Qods Force on certain occasions -- further evidence of the high level of coordination between Hezbollah and the Iranians on Iraq.

Since American and multinational forces withdrew from Iraq, Unit 3800 has been put to work elsewhere in the region, primarily in Yemen. There, Hezbollah and Qods Force personnel have helped the Houthis, a Zaidi Shiite insurgent group, fight the government. Reports from the Treasury Department and the New York Times indicate that Hezbollah and Qods personnel coordinated their operations in Yemen, with the former in charge of transferring funds and training Shiite insurgents, and the latter in charge of transferring advanced weapons such as antiaircraft missiles. U.S. intelligence agencies detected these activities, which led former White House counterterrorism advisor John Brennan to state in October 2012, *"We have seen Hezbollah training militants in Yemen and Syria."* National Intelligence Director James Clapper reinforced this point in his January 2014 "Worldwide Threat Assessment," noting that *"Iran will continue to provide arms and other aid to Palestinian groups, [Houthi] rebels in Yemen, and Shia militants in Bahrain to expand Iranian influence and to counter perceived foreign threats."*

Besides branching out to Yemen, Unit 3800 received another boost to its capabilities and prestige in 2012, when Hajj Khalil Harb -- a longtime Hezbollah commander and close advisor to Nasrallah -- was appointed to lead it. Harb is an experienced operative who has held various key positions, especially in terms of working with other organizations and overseeing special operations.

He served as deputy commander of Hezbollah's central military unit in Southern Lebanon during the late 1980s, where he gained his first substantial experience in special operations against Israeli forces. He later assumed command of Unit 1800, the Hezbollah force dedicated to assisting Palestinian groups by operating in the "ring countries" around Israel and infiltrating individuals into Israeli territory to conduct terrorist attacks and collect intelligence. According to the Treasury Department, Harb also traveled to Iran many times in his role as coordinator between Hezbollah, the Palestinians, and Tehran. After his role in Yemen became apparent to U.S. intelligence, the department designated him for sanctions in August 2013, citing his long body of work.

Appointing Harb to head Unit 3800 no doubt made a great deal of sense to Hezbollah's leaders given his experience working with other organizations, his close relations with the Iranians, and his expertise in special operations and training. The unit has likely benefited from his guidance and upgraded its capabilities since then. Deploying members of this unit to Iraq would also make sense given Harb's status as a former advisor to Nasrallah, who would presumably want an experienced commander in charge of such an important arena.

The war in Syria requires a great commitment from Hezbollah in terms of personnel and weapons, and significant numbers of its fighters have already lost their lives in helping the Assad regime. Yet given its willingness to answer Iran's call for help in Syria, the group will probably answer the call to fight in Iraq as well. Nasrallah is already laying the groundwork to justify such involvement by invoking the same hollow excuse of "defending Shiites and Shiite holy places."

As in the past, Hezbollah's contribution does not have to include hundreds of fighters, but only a limited number of experienced trainers and special operations "consultants." This type of contribution would not overstrain the organization, and it could facilitate far-reaching achievements for Iraqi Shiite militias.